KENYA

STORIES FROM THE MISSION FIELD

KENYA

STORIES FROM THE MISSION FIELD

KENYA

Stories from the Mission Field

COPYRIGHT © 2017
St Shenouda Press

All rights reserved. Except for brief quotations in critical publications or reviews, no part of this book may be reproduced in any manner without prior written permission from the publisher.

ST SHENOUDA PRESS
8419 Putty Rd,
Putty, NSW, 2330
Sydney, Australia

www.stshenoudamonastery.org.au

ISBN 13: 978-0-9945710-5-2

All scripture quotations, unless otherwise indicated, are taken from the New King James Version®. Copyright © 1982 by Thomas Nelson, Inc. Used by permission. All rights reserved.

Cover Design:
Mariana Hanna
In and Out Creation Pty Ltd
inandoutcreations.com.au

CONTENTS

Introduction	7
MAMA ONNIE AND THE FLASH FLOODS	9
MOVIE ON THE ROCKS	13
GOD WILL PROVIDE	17
I SAW JESUS	23
THE GOOD SAMARITAN	31
A CHANGE OF MIND	35
I WILL USE YOU	41
BRINGING THE RAIN	47
WHEN THE BISHOP ARRIVES	55
I WAS A STRANGER AND YOU TOOK ME IN	57
THE EXCORCISM	61
AFRICAN YOUTH CAMP	71
A SACRIFICE OF LOVE	77
THE CHICKEN AND PRAISE IN THE DARK	83
CANDY AND KIDS	87
MIRACLES IN PRISON	93
ESCAPING THE GRIP OF DEATH	101
THE ORPHANS	109
RESURRECTION GARDEN	113
AFRICAN SAFARI	115
SPONTANEOUS ENGAGEMENT	117
COW DUNG HUTS	119
MOUNTAIN CLIMB	121
SHARING JESUS	123
THE BOOK OF ACTS RE-LIVED	125
ELEVENTH HOUR SALVATION	129

Introduction

"The generous soul will be made rich, and he who waters will also be watered himself."
Proverbs 11:25

Since the apostolic era the Christian church has been active in reaching out to all people and delivering to them the message of salvation, our Coptic Orthodox Church continues this mission to this very day.

One of the most active missionary service of our Coptic church is that of Africa. Guided on this missionary service by His Grace Bishop Paul, various youth went out into the streets, homes, churches, market places, prisons and orphanages reaching out to all and sharing with them the unfailing love of Christ and His gift of salvation. The youth were blessed to be part of the ongoing services of the Coptic Church in Africa, accompanying various fathers, deacons and servants in the many services they perform both pastorally and evangelically.

The following stories are recounts written by various youth from all over Australia who were blessed to take part in this service and returned to share an abundance of experiences and spiritual benefit.

We pray these stories will be a source of spiritual benefit and a means of encouraging more youth to venture out of their comfort zone and gain African experiences of their own.

MAMA ONNIE AND THE FLASH FLOODS

It started out as any other morning. After having our usual morning "Mama Onnie African orban" (MOAO), we were called out to help in the local village. Mama Onnie is a very special lady. On a daily basis she awakens at 4 am to walk for 2 hours to her local church morning service. Luckily for us it was next to the hospital accommodation we were lodging in. After service she would make her way down into our common area and bake us the sweetest loaf of bread, which tasted exactly like orban from St. Mark's church in Sydney, hence the name.

Being in Johannesburg, South Africa, was very different from the usual societal and hospital settings we were used to back in Newcastle. The people here were so impoverished that at times it felt selfish to even think that we were hungry, cold or lacking in anything.

After being picked up from our accommodation by Fr. David (the local Coptic priest) we made our way to a village just on the outskirts of town. The scenes we drove into would change the life of even the hardest of hearts. Heavy winds and flash flood storms had ripped the roofs off the huts of the locals. As the rain continued to fall with extreme volume, you could see their belongings slowly starting to degrade from damage or float in a newly made indoor puddle.

With great foresight, Fr. David brought big tarps with him to help cover the gaping roofs while we slowly started to amend the damage one by one. But this was no ordinary S.E.S (State Emergency Service) like project. As we started covering up their huts, what they did brought absolute shock to all workers. There was no sighing, wailing or crying. There was no blaming the high heavens and screaming in anger to the Man in the heavens who created and controls all things. Instead, smiles. As we started to use the tarps, there was happiness. Singing even! They began to sing what we commonly know as the Trisagion (Holy God, Holy Mighty, Holy Immortal). The sound erupted through the street as each section joined in, all in one accord and while lifting their hearts to the Lord. How can this be that they lose everything, and yet still be so content and complete with what they have? This touched all our hearts, and though I didn't know the hymn in their local language, it didn't stop me from trying to catch it and sing along (and in the process probably say a few heretical things, judging by the looks I was getting).

Coming home that evening we were all quiet on the bus as we contemplated in amazement the events that had just passed. Saddened by what happened and worried about medical issues I was facing at the time, Mama Onnie's radiantly beaming face was a sight for sore eyes. She saw us as her own children. Sensing that I felt disturbed by everything going on, she sat me down in the lounge and asked me of my troubles. I began to dissect to her all that was weighing me down inside. In my weakness, I secretly believed that these problems were much too complicated for her and that she would not have any kind of solution for me. However I didn't want to disrespect her by brushing her off and I also really appreciated the gesture of her caring for me.

After letting me finish my story in its entirety, and 3 slices of "MOAO" (her solution to all life's problems) she walked away without a word. Not the response I was expecting, I began to think not so nice things towards her in my native Egyptian tongue. But before I could even finish off the "sheteema" (unkind word spoken in frustration), she returned with a bible in her hand. She quickly opened up to a verse in her Bible, which looked like gibberish to me. However it was quickly made known to me that she was reading Matthew 6:27,

"Which of you, by worrying, can add one cubit to his stature." This took me by surprise, perhaps more than the events earlier in the day. How can this be! What unwavering faith. How can someone who suffers like the locals, have such an unconditional love and faith in our Master. And I, who am blessed with everything and every sign indicating that God blesses my life, am often blinded to the fact.

With a giant hug and one final slice of "MOAO" I got up and went into my room to pray. It had been a very eye and heart opening experience of a day. One that moved me to go and thank Him for absolutely everything I once took for granted. This is a typical day in the service of people in Africa. TRY IT!

MOVIE ON THE ROCKS

It was a warm evening as the sun began to set from the blue Tanzanian sky. We all hopped onto the bus, one by one, enthusiastic to watch with the local people, The Passion of the Christ - the movie that within a scarce 2 hours, summarized Jesus' lifetime: his coming, his purpose, his miracles, and his death and resurrection. Our zeal hardly kept us on our seats, clapping and dancing, singing hymns, and praising God. Despite the language, English or Swahili, we were thanking God with all our hearts. Although we had a little amount of sleep due to early mornings and late nights, we never got tired. A constant energy pumped through us, God blessing all that we did. The bus ride was the place where everyone could meet together, and could share what we all have in common-our love for Christ. The journey felt so short; before we knew it, we had arrived.

We had found the perfect location: a bustling marketplace full of people. There were stalls everywhere, selling groceries, poultry, fish and other foods. The ground was flat, with large masses of rocks scattered randomly. Seeing us foreigners, people everywhere were attracted to the area where we were setting up for the movie. The local people kept asking us questions about what we were doing, and were ecstatic to hear that we were setting up a movie, due to films being such a big part of their culture. Crowds began to gather waiting to see the movie, but as time passed impatience began to flood over the people from the long wait. Complication had risen, the marketplace was just too busy: there was nowhere the projector would fit, especially with all the wires and connections that were needed in order to play the movie. Gradually, people began to leave. If only those mounds of rocks hadn't been there then there would have been ample space! We huddled together to pray - God wouldn't let all the people down! As we asked God to show us the way, someone came up with a suggestion-we could put the projector on one of the rock piles! We were unsure of whether it would be stable, but, it was our last resort and so it was worth a try. It fell off a few times, but then we used the rocks to put weight onto the projector and make sure it stayed in place. Soon enough there was silence, despite the mobs of people. Everyone was intrigued by the movie. Miracle after miracle, the people would put their hands together at the amazing wonders of God. The rock hills became a blessing, lifting up the screen so that even more people could see it, and the rest of the mounds were used so that people could sit on. We thanked God for resolving the problem; although this miracle was not as obvious to the eye as the ones in the movie, we could still see God working in our lives.

The following morning, we woke up bright and early to spend some quiet time with God on a beautiful beach. It was extremely tranquil and peaceful; it was silent except for the gentle hush of the waves. It was obvious to see God's hands at work-he created every wave, every grain of sand. It just went to show how carefully and delicately he made this earth. Later on in the day, we went for visitation, going around to the huts of the local people. We passed a gigantic natural sculpture made of boulders, contemplating on this we could see how big some of the things God made were. As we entered the cramped spaces, we came to the realization of the people's lifestyle in comparison to our luxuries. They had so little, yet were so content. We have so much more, yet are never satisfied. Every house we visited, we always told those who lived there to be grateful for what God had given them, yet we could see that we were definitely not practicing what we preached. They could see God's work around them and could feel his presence through the creation of God, but our destruction of nature and replacement with man-made things has erased this reminder from our society. This prompted me to remember how great our God is, He created the big and the small, and He is seen in his creation, even in the people around us, the plants and flowers, the wildlife. God is clearly seen in the ordinary things, if we want to see Him.

GOD WILL PROVIDE

I glanced one last time at the crowd of anxious parents waving goodbye as we disappeared behind partition into customs. My mind was disturbed with conflicting thoughts of excitement and weariness "what am I doing with this group? Do you really think you'll see God on this trip? The group is so big I doubt it will be of any benefit? People are already asking dumb questions. These thoughts continued to prevail...

As I took my first step into Nairobi, Kenya, I was not surprised by the thick smog of brown polluted air. The smell of tossed garbage and the herds of cars and men engulfing arriving passengers. I was one of the stragglers, walking on my own, being one of the last to get off the plane and hurried onto the bus awaiting our arrival. I felt lonely and overwhelmed. The bus ride was bumpy, the group was loud and rowdy, people shouting and taking selfies (I was not very impressed, judgemental thoughts ran through my mind). Although I was surrounded by people I felt removed as a boat lost at sea. I lifted my heart to God "God I have no idea what I am doing amongst this crowd, I don't know half the people, I feel lonely. Please comfort my heart and allow me to see your hand. Please let me benefit from You on this trip." I fell asleep.

I woke to the squeaking of aged breaks as the bus halted. We were in the confines of the monastery. The monastery was vast, in the centre was the pooling area for cars rushing patients in and out of the hospital. To the left was Saydena's headquarters, where he welcomed us and explained the itinerary for the trip. As we sat together with Sayedna, people were laughing and talking as the excitement of being in Africa finally sunk in. Sayedna tried to settle us down but the group was chatty. He raised his voice and finally got everyone's attention. With his fiery bright blue eyes he asked "why did you come to Africa? What do you think you'll benefit? No one replied, everyone eyes darted to their feet, praying that Sayedna's fiery gaze would not be set on them. At this silence Sayedna asked "do you even want to be here?" He began to explain to us "guys, every year a group like you comes from America, Canada, Australia etc. All with the same mindset- I want to come to Africa to have fun, take photos with a black kid and put it on Facebook. This is not service and if you think this is the real Africa you are wrong. You think that you come to Africa to serve but in actual fact you are the ones who are being served. Trust me you will learn so much from these people, they have nothing yet are so happy. Please my children, be serious about this trip, spend time with God, he loves you and wants you to be filled with his joy. Be honest and mark my words you will be transformed. Any sin or problem that you have, confess it here in Africa. Don't worry we are not your priests from Sydney, we won't remember, we don't know you, go to the Lord with all your burdens and be cleansed, allow God to start fresh in your life."

Sayedna's words felt like a Band-Aid being torn off a dirt filled wound. He was causing us to expose our sin, the dirt that had been hiding beneath a mask, constantly infecting our wounds. Everyone was silent. It seemed like everyone was deep in thought. At Sayednas words I began to look within and realize that my attitude at the start of the trip was wrong. Who was I to judge the people on the trip saying that they are asking dumb questions and being here for the wrong reasons- we all have sins and problems, some of us are better at dealing with our issues than others. At the end of the day we were all on this trip for the same reason- To experience the mighty hand of God. How could I judge weather I would experience God based on the size of the group. I began to realise that I needed to change, I needed to sit with God, expose my sins and allow him to fill me with His love. I sat in the chapel and Gazed at the floor length painting of our Father. With paper and pen I poured out my deepest concerns burdens hopes and fears.

Towards 5pm a few of us congregated in Saydena's headquarters and pulled out a few hymn books and started singing. Slowly other people began to trickle into the room and join until all 40 of us were present. Sitting in a circle, with the guitar playing, everyone praised joyously. It was truly incredible! It is so difficult to describe the aura, but it felt as though the room was overflowing with love, there was an unspeakable connection as everyone sang in unity. Our voices even trailed beyond the confines of the headquarters causing people to walk in and see what was going on. Sayedna and Abouna walked in hearing the praises from outside and joined in. These hours of singing were memorable to all. Everyone agreed that the talk by Saydena earlier in the day had impacted us all, changed our attitude, encouraged us to sit with God and be filled with His love.

Later during the trip I witnessed what Sayedna said in the talk, that we would learn from these people that have nothing, yet are so happy. We went out on visitation by foot. Singing hymns we walked through the untamed grass and orange dry dirt of the villages; Cows were tied to trees, a sign of established living; young girls were spotted balancing large bucket of water on their heads, while others were taking turns in manually pressing water through the well. It honestly felt like we were living in the time of the bible, where Jesus walked the villages by foot, no technology no fancy cooking, everything was reliant on crops and livestock. As we continued to burrow closer into the village, we arrived at a small mud house, with no animals parked at the entrance. An elderly women with a lame leg greeted us and warmly welcomed us into her humble abode. The 5 of us sat in what was the bedroom, kitchen and lounge. The mattress in which the lady slept on was the couch we sat on and the kitchen was at the base of the mattress partitioned by a curtain. The elderly lady urged us all to take a seat and immediately left us to bring out some food. Her leg was lame and she was having a hard time getting round, we urged her not to trouble herself with food but she insisted saying "You are my guests you have come all the way from Australia to visit me, how can I let you come to my house without feeding you?" As we sat together we read the bible and later discovered that she lost her husband 1 year ago, the sole provider for the house. Also, due to her lame leg she could not do much work, or travel to get food and did not have enough money to own livestock, let alone the health to maintain them. We asked her how she gets food and sustains living, her response "God provides, he always take care of me." I really felt embarrassed at her words. I felt smaller than a grain of sand. I have everything, my own room to sleep in, a couch that is not my bed, constant supply of food, family, health and still I complain and do not trust that God is taking care of me; while this women really has nothing, she does not even know if she will eat tomorrow- yet she has everything, she is filled with Christ, having full trust that He will provide.

I SAW JESUS

I want my story to be anything but cliché. Yes, I was spiritually weak before Africa and I had this big revelation over there and now that I'm back, I feel I know my purpose in life and I know Christ etc. Going to Africa was so much more than that.

I currently study a Bachelor of Dramatic Arts, which is theatre as such. I study acting, directing, producing, stage-managing, basically everything you need to become creative in the theatre industry. I grew up idolising the glamour of Hollywood and all its big names. From Audrey Hepburn to Dakota Fanning, I envy that they do what they love on such a global scale. It was safe to say that I was living in two worlds and I knew which world I wanted to be a part of more. Apart from myself and another boy, no one in my grade was Christian or a practicing Christianity and I hated talking about religion in front of them. When it came to church on Sundays, I had no interest in putting away my creative side to be taught how to be humble and Christ-like in everyday life. Yes, you can clearly see I hardly cracked open my bible, let alone prayed.

When I first heard about this Africa trip back in the beginning of the year, I kept thinking about it. It was constantly on my mind and my sister, who had been previously, kept telling me I should do it. Another friend of mine, who goes to the same church as me, said to me that she was a hundred percent in and we should all do it together and it would be a new experience. Eventually I agreed. There was this one musical, however, that I had wanted to a part of all year and it so happened that the rehearsal dates fell on the times we would be in Africa. I called up my friend and cried to her and kept saying that God knew how much I wanted to audition for this musical, I love it, why did it have to fall on the dates of Africa, I don't even want to go Africa etc. So you can see how pretty unmotivated I was to go to this unknown country, in the middle of God knows where, to do God knows what. I was also more afraid of the person I would be when I came back. What if I have this major life changing experience and I become super holy and all my friends think I'm insane? What would happen at uni? Would I even want to keep studying theatre anymore?

I was angry. I didn't care that people of past years were

telling me that I would love it. I knew I wouldn't and by the fact I had to take eight different vaccinations for all these various diseases, I was convinced God was sending me to Africa to die. Ultimately, the date of the flight crept closer and I had no choice but to accept my actions and just be positive. It was a new experience and who knows what could happen there!

Arriving in Nairobi, I didn't realise how similar to Egypt it was, except it was a lot less dusty. That first night was our first night of serving. After lunch, though, I wasn't feeling right. My stomach was twisting and aching and I knew there was no way in the world I was going out with them to serve. It was only the first night and I was already sick! Seriously?! It felt like I was already so frustrated at being there, everything was different and God was not helping at all. Why was I even there?

I remember it took me a while to stop blaming everything on God and to start taking responsibility for myself. I know that God put me here for a reason, but to know what it was, I had to wait and be patient. That day came along after our excruciating ten hour drive from Nairobi to a small town named Maseno. Then, I entered into what I can only describe as the biggest roller-coaster ride of my life. I had realised something. I was sad because seeing the way the Kenyans live and the fact that they're so poor used to break my heart. I spoke to one of my friends back in Australia and was telling him that I was upset that some of these people will never get a chance to see the world and don't know that there's so much more out there! My friend replied by saying that, "at the same time, there's nothing too far behind them. Their lives are pretty constant on a day to day so they can live in the moment without realising it". It was such simple words but it had a huge effect on me. I stopped seeing the Kenyans as these poor, unfortunate people, but just as people, whose lives, in most ways, are simpler than mine will ever be.

Then I saw Christ for the first time probably in my entire life. Not in a mass, or by praying or anything fancy. I've heard about Him, I know about Him, have I felt Him? Yeah, maybe. But have I seen Him? No, never like this. We were doing house visitations one day, which means you and a few fellow Australians and a Kenyan deacon, who helped translate for us, went to various Kenyan homes and spoke to them about Christ. That day I only had one other Australian with me, a deacon and a Kenyan priest, Father Bishoy. I saw Christ while sitting with the Kenyans; outside in such gorgeous weather, with Father Bishoy talking to them. We sat down with a family of about ten and they were such a lively bunch of people. They were nodding and smiling along with what Abouna was saying to them. I had no idea, it was all in Swahili but I was so mesmerised. I would look around them all and I could see Christ sitting next to us on the floor, or one of the chairs. Then abouna would translate what he said from Swahili to English and the words he was saying was just so knowledgeable and he made you see verses in different ways. He really knows his stuff! And what do I know? Basically nothing compared to him. Abouna looked over at me and my fellow Australian and told us that he loves telling stories and in everything he does, he loves to make people laugh. My heart just broke and I was almost in tears. It was simple companionship between us and the house we visited and it was peaceful. Everything I needed in my life, coming from such a busy world.

The next day was the day God decided to give me a wakeup call. We visited a women's prison in the morning and I was really hesitant at first. All I could picture was big, bulky women with shaved heads and tattoos up and down their arms. Basically what a female prisoner in a Hollywood film looked like. I am dead serious when I say they were they kindest, most peaceful and happiest human beings I had ever met in my whole entire life. We shared things from the bible first, whoever had something to share, did. I didn't because I was terrified to stand up and speak to them about Christ. Then came the hardest part. Anyone who was sick and/or needed Abouna to pray on them came to the front and knelt down. Right where we were sitting. I found myself getting weirdly teary. I've seen Abouna pray on dozens of people before! What was happening? Before I knew it, I couldn't hold my tears in anymore. I sat behind one of my friends and balled my eyes out. Seeing these women who have nothing, who are in there for silly reasons, some of whom will face the death penalty, kneel down and bow their heads to Christ, it was such an indescribable feeling. These women are in prison for Pete's sake and here they are talking to the Abounas confessing their sins, wanting to be healed, how does that make me feel? I look at my own life and think what on earth I was even doing with it before I came here. God knocked me on the head and said, now do you know why you're here? Now do you realise how much bigger the world is than you?

A couple of days later, we were told by Sayedna that we were going to Tanzania to preach there. He also clearly mentioned that it was a Muslim country and that we were going to be preaching in their houses and on the streets and basically anywhere in the open where we could be killed instantly! Our first night upon arriving there, we were told we were going to some random market to show 'The Life of Jesus' movie. Doing that in a predominantly Muslim country? Yeah, no thanks. Yet I went along anyway.

One of the Kenyan deacons that came to Tanzania with us kept announcing we were showing Jesus' movie and everyone was staring at us. I had never been so scared. When we got off the bus, Sayednea asked us to form a prayer circle, with all us Australians, and he asked God to at least touch their hearts and make Himself known to them. At that moment, I felt this calm upon me and I knew it was the Holy Spirit within me telling me not to be afraid. For the first time that night, I smiled genuinely and not nervously. We walked a couple of metres away from the bus and the deacons went off to set up the projector. Looking around and seeing the dark-skinned Tanzanians staring back at me was kind of freaking me out. I began doubting again, the movie wasn't loading and I was just waiting for the Police to arrive or someone to open fire or someone to come from behind and stab me.

At first, the responses were mixed. There were a few rowdy boys in the back scoffing at the screen and talking loudly. It made me so uncomfortable, I clung myself to one of my friends. The movie finally started to play and I began to calm down again. The viewers even clapped at Jesus' miracles! The movie attracted at least 150 people. When the movie had finished, Sayedna gave a short prayer and word and we all hopped onto the bus again. We had to do this every night but I grew more confident every time. Isn't that why I was there? To be still and not afraid? To be a beacon of the Light for the world?

All in all, it was a definitely a life changing experience. Would I do it again? In a heartbeat. I really want to say that it's ok to not know Christ before going. I didn't. It's so scary because you are asked every day to read your bible and to share from it too. But this trip gives you purpose. You may not know it during the trip, but later, because if I learnt anything it's that God works according to His time. Unfortunately, that means you do have to be patient.

My whole life I've wanted to adopt children from around the world and give them a home and introduce them to Christ. Maybe become a foster parent, who knows, but going to Africa made me see that I have the ability to achieve so much more with my life. And it's something you never stop think about. And though since coming back, I may still not be the most spiritual and sometimes I'm too lazy to go mass or I don't always read my Bible, I will never take the simple things in my life for granted. Very cliché I know, but the fact that I have my own room, or a roof over my head, or the fact I can go to a shopping centre and buy clothes that I like!

I know me.

I know my mission in life.

I know God.

THE GOOD SAMARITAN

Part of the service in Maseno was that we were to go to the market and preach to the public every Monday. This involved a group of servants and Kenyan deacons going in groups to the local markets, visiting each stall and spreading the Gospel to all. On this particular occasion, it was the third time I was to go to the market with eight other servants - a larger group than the two people I had gone with the first two times. Being the third time I went to the markets, I thought that I would not benefit anything because I had done it a few times already and I went with this negative attitude.

After walking a few kilometres we arrived at the markets and as we entered the markets there was a man lying face down on the main road. His clothes looked as if they had been immersed in mud and were torn to the point that they were not wearable anymore and he had no shoes on his feet. We were walking in pairs and I was at the front of the group with the deacon. As we approached the man I recognized the man from my previous visits and I knew that he was a drunkard and that he was probably drunk again. As I approached the drunken man I walked straight past him without thinking twice and all the other servants followed me, except one of the older servants who had fallen behind the group by a few metres. When that servant saw the man lying flat on his face on the road from afar, he literally ran to him, turned him over and started to try and get him to regain consciousness. It was then that we turned around and saw that one of the group members had the man in his arms trying to help him that we all realized we needed to help mainly out of guilt. Some of the group went to get the man some water and milk to help him, while others carried the man to the side walk were they sat him upright as he regained consciousness.

What was amazing was that not only did the member of the group help the man, but he refused to leave him sitting on the side walk alone until the he had ensured that the man was well. After the drunk man regained awareness, he was so moved by the great act of kindness of the member of the group that he was in tears even though the servant did not preach to him any message except that he said "Jesus loves you" repeatedly. When the servant that helped him told him that God still loves him regardless, the man that was drunk began to inquiring about God. The servant insisted that he accompany the drunken man to his home in order to ensure that he is well and rested. However being in a foreign country it was not safe for him to go alone, so he paid for the drunken man's taxi ticket after instructing the taxi driver to take him straight home.

It was at that point that one of the servants pointed out that we had all neglected this man, but our friend has acted exactly like the Good Samaritan. The actions of that servant on that day not only touched the heart of the drunken man and may have possibly altered his ways, but it brought us all to the realization that Christianity isn't just a title but a lifestyle. We all saw the man lying there but we walked straight passed him without caring. But that is not what Christ taught us and it was shameful that despite the great love Christ has always continued to show us we were not able to reciprocate it to everyone else.

This servant saw the Christ in this man, even though he was drunk, and he did not cease to help him knowing that what he was doing was not to the man but to Christ. Ultimately that is how Christ lived, he came to save all and He did not show partiality and it really hit home how we had done just that. It also showed how bad company can corrupt good habits and that by one person walking past we all followed even though we knew we should help. Also on the other hand, it showed us the impact that one holy man can have on a group of people and how his actions although he did not intend, had awoken us all from our selfish ways.

A CHANGE OF MIND

On this Africa trip, it was planned that we were going to stay in Kenya for 3 weeks. Kenya is a beautiful country once you settle in and meet the African priests and all the cool deacons. By the time we had hit the end of the second week, I was still pretty excited that we still had one extra week left with these beautiful people. On the day before the Apostles feast, we had just finished a long day at visitation and all the Sydney-siders sat in a room to eat with Sayenda, and he suddenly goes to the group "Ya walad (children) listen to me, I have an announcement! The Holy Spirit is talking to me and He is telling me that we need to go visit Tanzania for a week. He wants us to go and serve there. I think we should leave tomorrow night, what does everyone think? But be warned, Tanzania is not like Kenya, they are fanatical Muslims...this country is not like what you are used, and we are in the middle of the Ramadan, so it will be tough."

Everyone responded with such positive reactions except me. I was like "Whatttt!! No way! I love it in Kenya, I prefer to stay and I finally just got comfortable with everything....I don't want to start over again". I was also REALLY nervous that we were somehow now going to be sharing the Word of God to fanatical Muslims? This was SO out of my comfort zone, so I approached Abouna Augustinos about this – who told me that "if God has taken us THIS FAR in the trip, we're safe, we're healthy, we've seen about 1000 different transformations and miracles, you don't think He'll look after us in this country?" I was barely convinced, in my mind, I just did not think it would be a good idea. But Monday morning 4am came, and so did the long 9 hour bus ride where almost everyone in the group had some form of illness and was sitting uncomfortably on this ride. I remember thinking to myself, "God, there is nothing you can possibly show me in Tanzania that I couldn't see in Kenya." With that mind set, I arrived to Tanzania pretty negative. When we first arrived, we noticed the locals weren't nearly as nice as the Kenyans, and the compound we were staying in was not prepared to accommodate our number of people. Due to everyone being sick, the toilet was a very important room and even then almost all the toilets didn't flush. Before we knew it, a lot of us were already complaining to Abouna that we wanted to go back to Kenya. Abouna said to just give it a try and he was sure it would get better. We didn't listen to him, as a group, I knew a few of us were quite miserable, we felt like we were spoiled in Kenya, and to come here to Tanzania, it was like taking 2 steps back.

After day 3 we realised that we were in fact staying the whole week and we may as well start getting comfortable. I remember still telling God how uncomfortable and unhappy I was. I don't remember asking Him how he was. I remember telling Him that serving in this country where no one was reacting to anything we were saying, and to a church that was so empty, wasn't really helping us out in our mission trip. I remember His answer was silence.

A few days into Tanzania we had to preach on a ferry. The sun was extra hot that day and there were no free seats for us to sit on, most of us were standing and most of us were distracted. Yes, we still got up and sang, yes a few of us still got up and shared the Word of God with strangers on the boat who were listening, but I think we all knew that our heart was not in the service that day.... and this didn't go unnoticed, sayedna was very aware of our lax attitude. When we returned to the compound that day, we knew something wasn't right....Sayenda was not happy with us. Abouna spoke on behalf of him and said that we needed to sit with ourselves, and repent.

Repent? What did that even mean? Yes we hear in church over and over again to confess and repent and to confess and repent, but how do you sit with yourself without an abouna and repent? And what do we repent about? I couldn't understand, I was so confused.

The group naturally separated around the compound, everyone to him/herself, wondering what they had done wrong and how to fix whatever it was that went wrong.

It felt really quiet. Strangely quiet. Quiet enough to allow a new type of Voice to empower the negativity that grew and lived and breathed in my thoughts.... This new voice, was barely audible, telling me to open my Bible and do the Quiet Time of the day. That was no problem I thought, we've been doing Quiet Time for 2 weeks now....so I opened my Bible and started to read the verse for that day....and as I was reading though, something weird was happening to me. I am getting extremely touched by what I'm reading and it's making me really emotional. Before I know it, a tonne of sins in my past suddenly overtook my thoughts and I am shocked as to where they've even come from? Sins I have completely forgotten about – sins that I would've never confessed. I quickly grab a pen and paper and start to write them all down...it became more than what I thought and I felt so ashamed writing them down.

I looked at those sins and was speechless.... I didn't know what to think or say. Less than 2 hours ago I wasn't even sure what repenting meant, I thought I had nothing to even reveal, and now before my very own eyes I've got a never-ending list of sins that needed to be repented of! I just couldn't find the words to thank Him. I just needed to thank Him – but how do I thank Him after constant whinging for 4 days about how unsatisfied I was? How do I thank Him after reminding Him I would much rather be in Kenya then here?

Who would've thought I'd learn to the true meaning of repentance on this trip? Definitely Not me. If you told me I would come back with stories on songs, and performances I would say yes, I can see that happening... but to come back and to have truly understood what it means to repent? That I didn't see coming. But am I thankful for it? Boy, am I ever grateful. Thank you God - you opened my eyes in a way that changed the way I now view YOU - not just the world, not just the way I sin, but YOU. YOU were so loving to have given me this opportunity.

I WILL USE YOU

The first time I shared the word of God with someone, it went horribly. I didn't know what I was doing or what I was saying. "Just share a verse," they told me. I tried, but failed miserably. I just remember walking away thinking this kind of stuff wasn't for me. But that same evening, God was sending me a repeated message: I will use you. I didn't see how, but the message was so clear, and I believed it only because He said it.

The next day, I really tried to put in the effort, for His sake. It was something I just knew I couldn't do, but relying on His promise I decided to try again. I had a verse ready this time, and with my Bible on hand I left my room to find the rest of the missionary group before they left. When I arrived at the meeting place, I found no one. Perplexed, I wondered about the place and asked around but no one could help me. I eventually realized that everyone had left without me. By then I was upset. I found myself thinking: Lord what happened to what You said? I thought You were going to use me, and now this? In despair I told myself that I knew it was all really nothing.

I sat down on a bench and remember giving up at that moment. I just felt hopeless and useless. A moment past by as I wallowed in my self-pity when I noticed the man sitting next to me. He was a gentle looking man. His eyes fixed on my Bible. I found myself smiling as I said hi. He said hi back. Still he stared at my Bible. It soon started to get little awkward. Say something I thought to myself.

"Do you know what this is?" I asked.

"No," he said.

"This is the Bible," I said.

"Oh ok," he said as he strained his eyes. We sat in silence a little longer. I didn't know what to do. Say something I kept telling myself.

The words just came to me, "Do you want to share?"

Before I had even finished the sentence, the man's face instantly lit up. "Yes!" he remarked as he quickly straightened up and scooched over towards me to read.

By now my heart was racing, but I felt calm; I think by then I was already beginning to see what God was showing me. As we shared the one verse I had prepared, another man joined in to listen. I didn't yet understand the power of the word of God, that lesson was to come later, but relying on my own words and thoughts we continued to share from the Bible until I was suddenly cut-off with a question, "Which Church are you from?"

"The Coptic Church," I said.

"How can we join?" I nearly fainted. I couldn't believe this was real. I had just arrived into the country; I had no idea what to tell him! Holding back my excitement, I told them to wait while I found out, and ran to the priest to tell him what had just happened.

After it was all over, I entered the chapel, and before the altar I broke down into tears. His message was so sweet and clear: I will use you.

These were the first two days. I cannot begin to express all that I learnt on this mission trip. Suffice to say, my entire life has been turned upside down. Christianity is not a theory. It is life! It is real! Every single day, I could hear God's voice loud and clear. And I want to tell everyone; there is nothing sweeter on this earth, than to hear His voice, and to be used by Him!

Two weeks later I met the most amazing man. He was a Zambian priest, and he led us, a group of four people as we took to the streets and slums. We shared the word of God with everyone we met. I want you to picture Christ and His disciples walking through the streets, with masses of people surrounding them to hear the words of life! There isn't a better picture I can paint for you of what it was like. We were living the Gospel!

We walked and preached all day. It was only theory to me how the multitudes could go days without eating when they were with Christ (Mk 8:2), until that day. We felt no fatigue, no hunger and no heat of day. We were not ourselves.

It was about noon when Abouna pointed to a building we walked passed. "This is a brothel," he said. "And we have someone in there we need to save."

"What do you mean?" One of the girls asked. She was only twenty years old. And I was to learn so much from her.

"There is a woman, whose job is to change the bed sheets inside," Abouna explained. "This is her job, and she cannot afford to leave it. We need to get her out of this place." I tried to digest what Abouna was so calmly saying. "Can't the Church employ her Abouna?" I asked. Abouna nearly laughed.

"Well, let's go in." We all turned and looked at the girl who spoke. We all looked at her with bewilderment (including Abouna), until it was clear she was serious.

With a curious look, Abouna shook his head. He was the first to say it; "I'm scared."

"That's okay Abouna," she said, reaching for his hand. I couldn't believe what I was seeing. This gentle girl took Abouna's big hand in hers as she comforted us all. "No fear," she said. "Let's pray for them now." And we stood outside the brothel together and prayed. And then we went in.

As we entered, I continued to pray. Inside we met a group of twenty or so young men standing around a pool table. We soon learned that no one was working that day, due to a recent death of one of their colleagues. They were mourning. We mourned with them. I can't explain to you what happened, but God worked in the hearts of everyone that day, so that we soon found ourselves gathered and seated together, reading the Bible in a brothel! Abouna who was scared moments ago, I saw standing as a giant, as we shared the story of Lazarus'. And all around me I saw a strong desire for repentance in many faces. We walked in expecting to reach one person, instead the word of God reached the hearts of many that day.

Imagine if we had feared.

God wants to use you. He wants to lift you up above what you are. Above what you can do. Like St Paul the Pharisee, Moses who apparently couldn't talk properly (Ex 4:10), and even St Mary, whom God raised to be the

Mother of God! The saints are not something of the past. Christianity is the same today. We are to be the saints, if only we allow God to work in us.

God wants more for us than just the routine we go through day in day out that we sell ourselves to. We tell ourselves that there is no other way of life, that this is the best thing for us. Christ wants to make us complete. Just look at any character in the past who put God's will before their own.

Long story short: my life is not the same anymore. I have much to learn, but now I am beginning to realize just how much I have to learn. I am learning what repentance is. Do not fear. Book a ticket and go.

BRINGING THE RAIN

When I look back at the 3 weeks I spent in Kenya in 2014 I only remember an overwhelming sense of joy and thanks. My time spent in the church before going on this mission was minimal, I was really a 'Sunday Christian' – I attended the liturgy on a Sunday but my life was never filled with Christ till His grace moved me while in Kenya. If I had to point out the most amazing or inspiring thing I saw while there it would have to be the Kenyan people and the lessons I was blessed to learn from watching and being with them. Worship in Kenya is extremely different to what it is here in Australia. It's raw and bold and not dependent on having an ornately decorated building or even one made out of cement and bricks. In Kenya, the only element necessary to worship, to pray, and to celebrate the liturgy, is a heart full of love and yearning - something they have in an abundance I've never seen before.

One Sunday I was blessed to attend the liturgy in a very small, rural church. This church was made out of sticks and straw and its roof was made of tin, they didn't even have any flooring, beneath our feet was just dirt. Their altar was a small table we brought with us from the monastery we were staying in and there were no seats for the congregation, only a few benches. But the praise and worship I experienced and saw from them was inspiring. They were so full of thanks and joy and I could see how deep and enduring their love was for God and His church.

Our schedule while staying in Kenya was pretty intense – there was quiet time and then a morning prayer meeting and a talk followed by usually 5 or 6 hours of service then bible study and another prayer meeting and sometimes tasbeha later on. For a 'Sunday Christian' you could easily say I was well outside my comfort zone. This was all new to me. Christ was present every single day, fellowship was our bread and butter and service was truly a mission. When you enter a place like Kenya, especially in its more rural areas, and you leave the rest of the world behind, all that's left is what matters – God and His people.

"Finally, my brethren, be strong in the Lord and in the power of His might. Put on the whole armour of God, that you may be able to stand against the wiles of the devil. For we do not wrestle against flesh and blood, but against principalities, against powers, against the rulers of the darkness of this age, against spiritual hosts of wickedness in the heavenly places."

+ Ephesians 6:10-12 +

Before going to Kenya I kept hearing people say things like "you're going to see God's hand like never before", and I don't think I can do it sufficient justice using any words, but truly God's hand is so present in a way unlike I have ever seen. However, where God's hand is so present, the devil's hand, trying to undermine His amazing work, is so present too. My first visitation was really a testament to that. I was in a group of about 5 servants and we were accompanied by one of the Kenyan priests at a rural village where we walked for hours randomly visiting houses along the way. As soon as we stepped off the church bus a stranger, whose name we later learned was Maurice, approached us and was speaking to our Kenyan Father as if he knew him, but there was something immediately strange about it. This man was angry, upset and slurring his words. He would speak some chunks in English and then in Swahili, but none of it made any sense. I remember hearing him just spitting out random accusations against the Church and being so uneasy our Kenyan Father couldn't even keep him calm. He had tried to encourage Maurice to go his own way but he insisted on joining us and just wouldn't leave. I was scared. I remember feeling so uneasy – here I was in a remote village in Kenya where we had no access to any kind of communication or transport, walking along side a belligerent stranger who was yelling at us for no apparent reason, to random houses where we were supposed to share God's word. I looked around to the people I was serving with, fear was truly amongst us – it was unlike anything we had ever experienced.

As we approached the first house we were to visit, Maurice insisted on coming in with us. The fear followed us in. We opened our bibles to read and share but Maurice couldn't let us read His word without interruption. Every couple of verses we read Maurice would randomly yell out so viciously. The only thing I could hold on to was the Jesus prayer in my head "my Lord Jesus Christ Son of God have mercy on me a sinner and calm my fear." While Maurice stayed with us our entire journey, entering house after house, not letting us speak of God without interrupting us, slowly our fears settled, all we could do was trust in Him to bring us out safely – and He did. Just as God is real so is His enemy. And just as God's hand is so evident in Kenya, so was the devil's hand so evident. From that moment on we knew the kind of tactics we were up against, that we truly were there on a mission and that if we weren't diligent the devil would use all he could against us, just like he used fear during that visitation, to stop God's work.

> "Then the Lord appeared to Solomon by night, and said to him: "I have heard your prayer, and have chosen this place for Myself as a house of sacrifice. When I shut up heaven and there is no rain, or

command the locusts to devour the land, or send pestilence among My people, if My people who are called by My name will humble themselves, and pray and seek My face, and turn from their wicked ways, then I will hear from heaven, and will forgive their sin and heal their land."

+ 2 Chronicles 7:12-14 +

The diligence we needed to serve Him while we there was something that we lacked for a while. We were about two weeks into the mission and had exactly 7 days to go when we were given a talk by Sayedna that would completely shape the rest of our service, both in Kenya and back at home. It seemed like a normal morning, we met at the upstairs chapel for a prayer meeting and a talk before breakfast, only this morning was much different. Sayedna was upset with us, and with our efforts in our service and prayer lives. He told us that there was something wrong with our group – that we had no zeal, no fire. We were running late to masses and bible studies and ignoring the need for quiet time. We weren't taking this mission seriously, and it showed. He told us that if we didn't see God's hand while we were in Kenya that we would never see it anywhere else. A Kenyan priest had also talked to Sayedna not long before and asked him "Sayedna, what's wrong with this group? They've brought no rain. They are not a blessed group". Sayedna went on to explain that whenever a mission group came to the monastery they brought with them an abundance of rain, without fail, every group brought rain - and in Africa rain meant blessing. But we had been there for two weeks and there had not been a single drop. He told us it was because we weren't being serious in our mission. That truly we were here on a mission - to bring God's glory and God's word to an apostolic world - where preaching and healing happened every day. Such a mission needs fervent, diligent, purposeful prayer - and we were lacking in it.

The mood in the air had completely shifted after that hour. Girls were crying; boys were hanging their heads in shame. Only silence persisted. I remember I sat by myself for at least an hour reading and having quiet time. The rest of the group did the same. We spent that whole day in the monastery – praying, sharing bible study, and sitting quietly. Where there were people there was prayer and He was truly in our midst. That was the first and last day we had not been taken out to serve.

At about 3 or 4 am the next day He answered us - rain fell the whole day - pouring and soaking. We remembered the words of Sayedna and understood the power of prayer. We were asking Him to give us another chance, to bless the rest of our trip so that we might be able to serve Him and His people with all His power, and He replied. We turned to Him and humbled ourselves that He might hear us and He did.

I didn't hear about this next part until after I arrived back home, but it moved me even more and truly cemented how awesome and how powerful prayer is. It moves Him, and He moves mountains... That night a group of boys, who were led by one of the Kenyan priests, had decided that they would continue their prayers throughout the night. They took hour shifts and one by one through to the early hours of the morning one of them would rise to pray and then awake the next one when they had finished. When it had come to the last boy to pray, as he was praying, he woke the person next to him and said "wake up, wake up, do you hear that?!" The sound they were listening to was that of pelting rain that we all awoke to that day.

WHEN THE BISHOP ARRIVES

I travelled with a big group to Kenya in July 2014 and the whole experience injected into us joy and purpose. Because our group was so large, we were split into smaller groups of about 8 each. Each group would get off the bus in turns to their destination and on this particular day, our group was the last to get off. We went to pray the Liturgy in a very small village surrounded by numerous plantations. The whole liturgy was filled with life from beginning to end, each hymn, each response was sung in such a way that would uplift us all. It was towards the end of the Liturgy when an announcement was made that Bishop Anba Boules was coming to visit – what happened next is very touching.

The whole congregation left the building of the church and walked down the road – a distance of about 700 metres to greet the bishop (this was because his car could not travel on this narrow road leading to the church). On their way, each would cut a portion of a leaf from a nearby tree, some would cut palm branches and take them. I personally stayed at the church watching all this unfold from a distance. They led a procession for him, from the start of the road to the church – singing hymns and praising God for his visit. Does this sound familiar to you? To me it was as if Palm Sunday was being replayed for me live! Such joy, such simplicity in the people. We then entered the church where the bishop concluded the Liturgy.

After a long day it was time for us to head back and because we were the last to get dropped off, we were the first ones to be picked up. I looked around to each of the boys in my group and saw them all tired and about to sleep in their seats. On our way we picked up a group of African ladies who needed a lift on the same way. As soon as they entered the bus and started singing some hymns – it was as if power and joy was injected into us. Each of us began praising and singing in a way I had never seen before. It was contagious, as soon as every other group came on the bus we spread this joy until the whole bus was singing joyfully as loud as they could – to such an extent that every time I watch the video here on my phone as a memory, the speakers are about to explode. Where else can this happen? Such is the nature of the place and the people.

I WAS A STRANGER AND YOU TOOK ME IN

Market preaching is one of the services where the servants go together in a group to the market. Once there, we break off into smaller groups of 3-4 and casually speak to people there about Christ. This usually entails sharing a short contemplation based on a verse from the bible, a Gospel parable and saying a short prayer before moving on to the next stall.

On the first day of service in Maseno we went market preaching. May God forgive me for the following, but as we arrived in the midst of the hussle of the market, I was apprehensive towards the locals. The stall owners, the buyers, those rolling carts and everyone around me. People brushing past in all directions.

I tried keeping to myself, not getting involved.

As we approached the market, there was one particular guy in the midst of the chaos that was an absolute mess! I remember thinking to myself in disgust "I definitely don't want to be touching him". He was lying flat, face down in the middle of the road. He had vomit dripping from his mouth and all over his face. His clothes were torn and scattered around him. Everyone was walking around him. There was at least an empty metre radius around him because no-one wanted to get close to him and I was the first to follow this trend.

We had a reasonably large group this time of about 10-12 people. Everyone did the same. We walked passed and looked back... Except for ONE man.

He stopped, had compassion on the guy on the floor and hailed people over for help. He was rebuked by local spectators, but despite this he called them over to help and they did. He tended to the needs of this individual. Sat him up. Cleaned his face. Clothed him. Bought him a carton of milk and spoke to him.

At this point, all the other servants and I were very ashamed and learnt a valuable lesson from this compassionate gentleman. He was a living example before us of Christ's words in the Gospel "for I was hungry and you gave Me food; I was thirsty and you gave Me drink; I was a stranger and you took Me in; I was naked and you clothed Me; I was sick and you visited Me; I was in prison and you came to Me." Matthew 25:35-36.

This situation also made many of us reflect on the story of Lazarus and the rich man in Luke 16:19-31. We neglected this man on the floor who was no different to Lazarus whom Jesus loved. We acted as cold-heartedly as the rich man, and rather than being there to serve, we heaped condemnation on ourselves.

THE EXCORCISM

We were incredibly excited yet equally nervous. Tanzania was our next destination and from the few stories we heard and the little research we gathered it wasn't exactly a holiday you would advertise on brochures. The night before, Abouna Mina was telling us a story about the "jingies". Apparently they are little ticks that dwell in puddles of water and mud, which was pretty much 90% of the country. These so called jingies bury into the bottom of the foot and somehow navigate their way into the bladder. That was one of the "101 deadly insects" in Tanzania according to one web page. Despite the lack of basic sanitation, insufficiency of basic necessities such as food and water, the absence of electricity and not to mention the insurmountable obstacle of no wi-fi or Internet for 5 days, our greatest fear was in front of our very eyes, the airplane. Comparable to a family sized sedan and no higher than a full-grown man the cardboard cut out barely stood there against the faint winds. Furthermore, to avoid the plane from submitting to its weight and tipping over, a rusted metal pole supported the tail of the plane. But what was hard to imagine was that it were these paper-esque wings that were going to keep us afloat several kilometers above ground. It was no wonder Sayedna, Anba Bola, repeatedly stressed the weight restriction. The night before we had to bargain for an extra kilogram of our luggage. Moreover, to keep our personal weight to a minimum we weren't served breakfast that morning. We were clinging to our 3 kg luggage, as our empty stomachs churned at the sight of what could have been the last time our feet would be grounded.

Despite all that lay ahead we were very excited. As we began to ascend in to the skies I noticed Anba Bola pull out his bible and begin to read. However, we weren't prepared to miss any of this. We were so animated and bursting with nervous laughter in disbelief of what took place. We continued our mischief until suddenly we noticed the pilots concern. We slowly became subdued to an unwelcoming alarm that sounded from the cockpit. The pilot looked slightly bewildered as he looked outside his side window almost as if he was in search of something. After fiddling with a few buttons and switches he turned to us and broke the silence that was only intermittently interrupted by the sounding alarm. "Guys we have a slight issue, the navigator isn't working", the pilot claimed. Distressed, we began pouring our hearts in prayer. The pilot pulled out what appeared to be a dusty map and began to manually navigate the plane back to the Kenyan airport. Thankfully, we somehow arrived safely. A great feeling of relief overcame our weary hearts. Anba Bola kindly asked for the priests to leave the plane and for us to stay back. Suddenly the nervous tension gripped our hearts once again.

He looked at us in utter contempt. He began speaking words that will always ring in my ears. He started off by saying "Very, very bad!" Then he continued, "Do you know why this little adventure just happened? It was the devil that intervened. That you yourselves invited onto the plane. That you yourselves allowed him to bring us back to Kenya. Don't you see the devil doesn't want us to go Tanzania, he is burning that we are going to spread the word of God. The thousands of people there are screaming Christ's name. But you, not one of you has pulled out a bible and read it. Not one of you did quiet time in attempt to communicate with God. Its as if you don't care." I remember feeling this slight regret that we landed safely. I felt so humiliated and so humbled, I couldn't believe the ramification of our action. I couldn't believe that we could be the very reason why so many people that looked forward to this were not going to hear the word of God. It made me think, how could have I trivialized such a great privilege that I was certainly not worthy of?

Thankfully, the plane was restored and the issue was

solved. Although I think the issue was never technical it was just our lack of commitment and understanding of the value of this missionary trip. We remained focused in prayer pleading for forgiveness and did not utter a word for the remainder of the trip.

We finally arrived to Tanzania and despite our expectation what we saw from birds' eye view was yet still astounding. The landing strip was a grassless clay patch that didn't look too welcoming. Small houses, made of the seemingly abundant clay, scattered around the landing bay. Picturesque mountains lay around the skirts of the untouched land. It was beautiful in its simplicity. A young boy holding what amusingly seemed to be table tennis rackets waved the plane in to a safe landing. We couldn't help but notice a community of people that stood next to an isolated wooden house, or the airport, that only grew in number. They stood there motionless like kangaroos stunned by a beam of light. They were almost in fascination by these white alien-like creatures that dropped in a flying vehicle from the sky. From the little we gathered already we knew it was going to be an interesting week.

After a scenic drive to what seemed like the tip of Mount Everest we arrived at the compound. What we witnessed on our arrival was arguably the most emotional situation I have ever come across in my life. Never really grasping what Anba Bola said, "thousands of people screaming out Christ's name", it became all the more clear what he had meant. Although it may have not been literally a thousand there were a multitude of people from young kids no less than the age of 4 to elderly woman who greeted us several hundreds of meters before the entry. They greeted us with songs, hymns, cymbals, drums and above of all smiles and laughter. It was a true sighting of pure and overwhelming joy. They ran beside the cars waving frantically to win over our attention. Collectively, they sang amazing hymns with such enthusiasm and exuberance. It was without exaggeration a reception fit for a king. We were in utter disbelief.

The words that Anba Bola spoke became all the more apparent. Questions that I had no answers to began to flood my mind. Who was I to be welcomed this royal welcome? What was it that put me on this side of this glass window? Was it my citizenship from a developed country? Or was it the bachelor degree that I effortlessly achieved? Profound emotions of shame began to overcome us as we each realized that it was nothing we had done but God's grace that we ungratefully received. What they possessed was not much more than the little clothes they wore but they need nothing more but God's love.

We attended the mass bright and early the next morning. We stood as deacons in a church built of clay and pinewood. As impressively sized the church had been, the space was yet not sufficient for the abundance of pilgrims that had come from the scattered villages that neighbored. The congregation grew by the minute in anticipation of the joyous occasion. It was unique in its structure. It was still the typical Gregorian mass but was coloured with a vibrant group of people dressed in green and white, the choir. The choir played an integral part to the mass, as they would sing the congregational responses with music and dancing that would traditionally be uttered in the accustomed tune. It was a beautiful unique addition to the mass that certainly lifted our spirits in praise.

When my eyes scanned the crowed intermittently it was just so admirable how deep and sincere they appeared as they wholeheartedly offered their prayers. The mass went on for a relatively long four hours or so but I can honestly say we felt no presence of time. The mass concluded with the congregation moving as close as possible to the altar kneeling before Anba Bola where he stood with a cross held up to the crowd for a blessing. It was an unbelievable moment that was so genuine and heartfelt as we all were spiritually uplifted in prayer, it was a taste of heaven.

The spiritually powerful moment was evident as one member in the congregation broke into distressful noises and violent fits. It was without doubt he was demon possessed. The scene caught the eye of humble bishop who took a priest with him and marched as the crowd parted and made way to the possessed man. Anba Bola said a small prayer and invited Abouna Angelos to continue the exorcism in which he modestly refused. Anba Bola continued with the exorcism and when the man had ceased shaking and opened his eyes, he was astonished and confused at what had just taken place. It did not take long before he came to a sudden realization of what had happened and began to cry in repentance. After the conclusion of the mass a table was laid before the congregation, with two plates. The congregation assumed one line and began drop something in the bowls. Some people dropped in one of the bowls and some in both bowls. But I couldn't see what it was as they had firm hand around it. When I asked what was happening. The Deacon replied, "This is their offering." "There are two bowls: one for gratitude and the other was an offering for a personal request. They are giving what little money they own, but for those who had no money they would give anything that they grew for example pineapple, avocado or even a goat". Their simplicity and strength of faith amazed me. Some were giving their week's wages with faith and undeniable hope that God was going to undoubtedly answer their requests.

It was another day of visitations and as fatigued as I was, I must confess, I was not looking forward to it. However we met one lady that day that really moved me with compassion. Daniel had just read a few verses on trials and tribulations and spent a short time thereafter contemplating the verses. It was difficult not to notice the simple and peaceful smile the humble lady had as she sat modestly being attentive to every word Daniel spoke. At the conclusion of the visitation the lady repeated numerous times that she couldn't express into words how happy she was for our visitation. It was such a deep statement that took us all by surprise. We barely spent 5 minutes there but she was incredibly grateful. It made me ponder upon all the different services that run on a daily basis at our church, purely aiming to strengthen my relationship with Christ by teaching me to imitate him, love him, and to serve him. Yet the times I had voluntarily missed them for one reason or another, none of them truly served a valid excuse. Although it may sound cliché it so uncanny how you take something as simple as Sunday school, or even a bible study meeting for granted, until you experience what it is like to be void of these privileges.

Joe and I decided to go for a walk around the neighboring suburbs. As we walked down the muddy path we couldn't help but admire the simplicity of the people that we came across. There were the men that pushed pineapples on pedal-less bikes, the woman that balanced a pot of dried Ugali on the crown of their heads, and the children that trailed behind us in fascination of our unique appearance. They all shared one thing in common: their humbling smile that had this really heart-warming glow about it you just couldn't help but reciprocate it. We were suddenly spotted by a man who had a tribe of goats leashed by a rope that was tied to both his arms. In a struggle to lift his bound arm to wave our attention he repeatedly called out "please come", inviting us in. Joe and I went in hesitantly realizing that there was a very clear language barrier. However, this didn't concern them they were just extremely jubilant for our visitation in hope for a blessing. We had nothing to offer them but a short prayer that they were so content with. To be invited to a home housed by such simple people and to share a prayer with them was such a rewarding feeling. But what was even more amazing was despite the language barrier and the fact that after all we were strangers to each other, we were brothers and sisters in Christ and we were simply united in Christ by a prayer.

AFRICAN YOUTH CAMP

While in Africa we were involved in attending many camps with Bishop Boules and the youth of St. Mark's church in Zambia. These camps involved a combination of spiritual activities, sports activities and prayer meetings.

On one particular youth camp with sayedna and the youth, the theme for the camp was "Live like no one else, do hard things". This was especially relevant to the youth of St Marks church as during this time the youth where being affected by external influences, school, friends & society, to conform to bad habits. These involved stealing (because they were so poor and couldn't afford food, they were encouraged to steal food from the markets like their friends to be able to eat), missing the liturgy on a Sunday morning to go swimming with friends, drinking alcohol etc.

Sayedna's talk and abouna Abraham's prepared workshops where founded on the idea of "living like no one else", being different and saying 'NO' to these influences.

On Saturday night after a full day of workshops and sports activities, Bishop Boules suggested we do a big spiritual prayer meeting with all the youth and the servants of the camp.

This prayer meeting was not like any we had attended before. While waiting for everyone to come to the church some of the youth in the church opened up and spoke to us saying how they find it very hard to say 'NO' to their friends. They feel that by saying no they will be rejected by their friends and have no one to turn to, so they usually agree just to please their friends and family and to help their situation of being poor.

Once all the youth had arrived, Father Abraham began the night with a very uplifting talk on practical ways to 'live like no one else'. He used the analogy of a farmer and his fruits. After a farmer collects all his fruits (eg apples), he looks into the basket and picks out the good (whether one or two) out of the whole bunch collected. This is the same with God and his children. We are Gods fruits, we are his representatives here on earth and at the end of time God will collect all his children (the same way the farmer collected all his fruits) and he will look at us and pick the ones who were different to the world, the ones who 'lived like no one else', the ones who 'did hard things' and followed the bible and the teachings of the church. Father Abraham used Matthew 25:31-33 as an example from the bible:

> "When the Son of Man comes in his glory, and all the angels with him, he will sit on his glorious throne. All the nations will be gathered before him, and he will separate the people one from another as a shepherd separates the sheep from the goats. He will put the sheep on his right and the goats on his left"

The youth seemed very motivated and excited to change their lives, to try and 'live like no one else & do hard things'.

All the lights were then turned off, candles were lit and the youth began to sing hymns. This was the most extraordinary uplifting time. The youth were not just saying words they were passionately singing with all their hearts. Two by two they would go up in front of the altar and kneel down before the altar and pour there hearts out with tears asking Christ for his forgiveness and making promises to God about how they would 'live like no one else', how they refuse to go back to the way they used to be living, that they would prefer to die of hunger and thirst then to steal and do anything that would upset God.

Between each hymn sung, one of the youth would pray

and their prayer would be like an open confession, openly admitting out loud some of the things they have done and begging Christ for his forgiveness and strength to help them change.

During the prayers, the church felt like it was taken from earth to heaven. The presence of God was really felt in each of us and His presence was felt in the church.

Christ's saying was truly evident "For where two or three gather in my name, there am I with them" (Matthew 18:20)

The church was filled with incense. Many times during the prayer the lights would all automatically turn off, as if the devil was trying to prevent this amazing transformation that was being done to the youth by the grace of God.

The environment of these prayers left each one of us amazed and speechless at the faith of these youth. Abouna Abraham encouraged each of the youth to make a change to kneel down before the altar and make a promise to God to leave behind all the things that used to be done on a daily basis and trust in him whole heartedly and to see Gods blessing. He also encouraged each of them to encourage each other and stand by each other especially when you see one of your brothers struggling with something.

By the end of prayer each of the youth had encouraged

each other to kneel before the altar and make a promise to God to 'live like no one else and do hard things'.

This taught us a big lesson, that our lives should be different to everyone around us. We should not conform to society and be pressured in partaking in events and situations that will make us upset Christ. If our brothers and sisters in Africa who have much less than we do are able to make a promise to Christ to 'live like no one else and do hard things', how much more should we do with all that we have.

On the following day, the youth spoke to us saying how they felt this camp has changed their life and how regardless of there situation, they refuse to do what their friends outside church encourage them to do.

Some of the youth joined us on our visitations the following day. And in each house we entered and spoke about Christ, the youth would speak about how Christ has touched their hearts through the camp and encouraged the residents of the house to come to Christ, to come to church, to trust God with everything, even the little they have and watch how God will bless.

Many a time the residents would fall into tears saying how they have longed for someone to visit them and give them the encouragement and speak to them about God and that the message read to them from the bible today was a direct message to them about a something they have been struggling with recently.

This really showed us that when Christ touches someone's heart he truly transformers their lives and uses us to help and encourage others to come to Him.

A SACRIFICE OF LOVE

Myself and three friends stayed in Kenya for three weeks in December, and were left with many memorable experiences and stories to share. I think the best aspect of Kenya was the love everyone gave so keenly and effortlessly. From the first day we arrived, we automatically felt like we were part of one big Kenyan family (with whom we are still in regular contact with over 6 months later). This love was so sharply displayed by the servants who dedicated their lives to the church in Kenya (from America, Egypt, Canada...), the Kenyan priests and deacons, the locals, and virtually every household or person we had interactions with. It was a completely different culture of loving others more than yourself and a zeal for Christ.

Within the first few days of arriving we became really close with those who were living with us at the compound. We were having lunch with one of the servants, and amongst conversation I casually commented on how I really liked the wrist bracelet that she was wearing. Almost naturally she took it off and strongly insisted that I keep it with me. A few days later I was having a conversation with a friend of mine from Australia about how I wish we had made special shirts to remember this Kenyan trip in the future. The very next day, apparently one of the servants had overheard me and insisted that she give me hers to remember them by. I later found out that that was the shirt that she had gotten from her first church trip to Kenya (several years ago), her only one that had obviously meant a lot to her. These are just small examples to show that giving was just second nature to everyone, regardless of the person's needs or wants, others were always put first.

A big part of the mission in Kenya was visitations. This is where we walk to a particular area (without notice or invitation), and go door to door to say a short message from the bible (we visited both Christians and non Christians). Looking back at the end of the trip I realized that not a single person was not welcoming to us and happy to hear the word of God. They all greeted us with joy, and always offered us tea and something small to eat (chapatti is the main native food).

One day a small group of us were on visitations to a place that was quite far away, so we were walking for maybe 10km through what seemed to be the jungle for me. After a while of walking I began to get a bit fatigued and frustrated. Added to my frustration was that we missed lunch back at the complex, we seemed to be lost, and to top it all off it began to rain. The servant with me smiled noticeably when it rained even harder, and when I asked her why, she said that there would be more blessings in the service if we had to walk through the rain. I didn't really think much of it and kept walking frustrated.

When we finally arrived after a long trip, we came to a house that was definitely unfit to live in (even by African standards). It was in the middle of nowhere, the whole house was maybe half the size of my room, the ceiling was dripping and it was just a mess. The woman of the house (who was a widow with 8 young children) saw us and ran to greet us. When she saw us she began crying intensely and kept saying in her language (Swahili), that Christ had came to visit her this day. We cramped into her small house and all sat down together and read a small message in the bible (the parable of the 5 loaves and two fish). When we were finished and ready to go she demanded that we stay and wait for dinner! We were expecting some tea and beans (if we were lucky), but the lady took what seemed to be her only chicken and animal (usually families have several chickens, some goats and a cow) and killed it right in front of us. She prepared the chicken and fed us, not touching the food herself or her children. Later on the way back

I was told that because of that action her and her family would probably go a week without food at all. All that I had given her was a small icon of Jesus...

Abouna told us on our first day of arrival that we shouldn't leave if we hadn't heard the voice of God on a daily basis. I was a little bit worried when he said this in full seriousness, as I know that God always speaks to us in a still small voice that regularly goes unheard. However it seemed that in Africa God was screaming to us through a megaphone, almost impossible to miss.

One of the many examples I had hearing God's voice was one day when we were walking through a particularly poor area. Being in Africa for a while, we were all used to the low standard of living and poverty everywhere we went. However, something that really shook me up was a young boy who had no pants and a torn up shirt 5 sizes to big, covering less than half his body. The condition of this boy made me feel that any minute now he would drop down and die. I was really disappointed with God and even began to rebuke him- 'how can you say that you love us, how can you call us your children, how do you leave people to die this way...' A few minutes later we went to a visitation and one of the youth with us gave his sharing on the bible verse 'if God makes sure that the birds of the air have food, how much more will he take car of his children'. The very next house we went to, we started off singing a hymn- 'Finest bread I will provide, till their hearts be satisfied'. Later on we went back to the complex and abouna was giving us a sermon on how blessings and reliance on God stems from poverty. I had received the message.

The stories and experiences we shared in Africa were endless. We saw both God and people in a completely different light. We went to serve, but were constantly being served much more. I pray that God continually shows us His strong arm in Africa, and that these experiences may be used to encourage others to go and see that the Lord is good.

THE CHICKEN AND PRAISE IN THE DARK

During our service in Zambia we were often asked to visit a village two hours away from the main cathedral. The village was beyond a clear example of being under the poverty line but we were always met with a cheerful song and smiling faces from the congregation.

This was our very first visit and Abouna Mark (African Coptic priest) joined us on this trip to the rural part of Zambia, known as Mongolie. During our visit we would travel by foot from hut to hut preaching and visiting the Coptic congregation and we would often be given mangoes as a sign of appreciation for the visit. The mangoes were usually the only thing that they were harvesting at that particular season, and would often last them to next season. While visiting we would come across an occupied home built out of bricks. Most homes in this rural village were huts made of straw and if you had enough money, then one made out of bricks but with no windows and only a straw roof. This village was poor to the point that the rappers and bottles we had food and drink in, they would recycle and use as bracelets and shoes.

This was our 3rd visitation and by that time we had shared a passage from the bible with most families and continued to do so with this visit. A very old lady bent down and extended out her hand to greet us and allowed us to enter.

We opened up the bible and this verse came up:

'For whoever has, to him more will be given; but whoever does not have, even what he has will be taken away from him'. Mark 4:25

Abouna would translate while we read, and as soon as we finished this particular verse the lady stood up and excused herself. By then we were worried and confused to what had happened or had it been something we said that offended her. We could hear in the background the lady screaming out (in her dialect) to what looked like family/workers to gather something. The lady came back after 5mins and said "I have accepted the word of

God, and today I will be giving you guys a Chicken". Her genuine and sincere smile giving us this chicken still remains as a clear image in my head to this day. We were still confused and quite obviously rejected her offer (we were fasting) nicely.

We sat and thought about what that lady had just done. Many families in that village would have 1 or 2 chickens throughout the year and it would be killed and eaten for a special occasion. So you can say the value of this chicken was like a car to us westerners. Her giving up this chicken would show that although she might have a brick home, and mangoes, this chicken was something very precious to her and her family. To the point that most people in the city even do not eat chickens or have chickens to eat, but this lady gave all she had for a few missionaries. The smile these people had when we would visit them and speak to them about God, was on another level. It was complete simplicity and happiness regardless of their current situation. We would often repeat this story to a lot of our friends, but the sincere smile and happiness the lady had on her face we could never explain.

During that same visit to the village, we stayed there 3 days and would finish visitations when the sun went down (no electricity) and would continue the process the following day.

During the first night Abouna had a great idea of singing hynms in literally the dark. We had four benches lined up just outside the church near the bush, and abouna would start a hymn and we followed along. We did this for awhile and throughout every hymn we would stop and share something nice together. To our surprise, while we were singing we could see people from the bush coming and sitting and joining in the singing. This was probably the most beautiful thing to see. Our voices were so loud that people from a far distance away could hear and wanted to join in this praise.

In this village not everyone was baptized, but only a few. So we could not distinguish who was or was not part of the church. It had become very crowded that we needed to take 2 extra benches to accommodate all the people that came and joined us that night. We kept going for quite a while, but abouna needed to stop because we had a mass to pray in the morning.

The people loved the hymns session so much that the following night when we decided we would have an early night and not repeat what we did. We would often hear knocks and shouts at the door of the church from the people, as they wanted to repeat the same praise session that we did before.

"If two or more are gathered in My name, I will be amongst them". I could honestly feel God's presence in this hymn session. We didn't need to visit them, or bring the bible to them, they came to us from the praising that they could hear.

CANDY AND KIDS

Imagine this: It's an ordinary day, you wake up extremely fatigued and you begin to prepare for a foreseeable hard day at work. You leave the house and arrive to work 10 minutes before your shift all before being yelled at by your boss for not being there earlier than required. But you don't let that get you down. You fight through, because face it, you're hard working, but your seemingly nasty boss refuses to grant you a much earned lunch break. You're hungry. Your thirst is indescribable. Your toil in this job makes it ever so difficult to refrain from insulting your boss and there appears to be no resolve to your surfacing "starvation" predicament. Fortunately, the day is over and you're convinced that today was the hardest day of your life, and more importantly, you simply don't deserve this. You deserve better. You're a Christian. Don't get me wrong, you're grateful for your job, but heck, with all your selfless services you participate in surely you deserve more, right?

This is a story that hits-home for many of you, and one that sure describes me. Now, this story is not aimed at bashing you with correct Christian morals, nor is it intended to make you feel overtly shameful for being ungrateful for the multitude of commodities God has bestowed upon you (well, maybe slightly), but fundamentally, providing a different perspective.

My adventure started in Keyna, Africa in the fall of 2013, and truthfully, I was initially unimpressed. My first steps on African soil were experienced with an amalgamation of emotions, with frustration and relief as the main participants. To me, there was nothing exquisite about persisting through 25 hours worth of flights in seats intended for children, complemented with subordinate flight service. The complaining doesn't stop there. The group and I were escorted in a beat-up van through conditions that accurately reflected my history studies of WW2. My regret became ever so evident and the prospect of leaving my hospitable, air-conditioned and spacious abode for this war trodden country was deemed uncalculated and idiotic. While these thoughts consumed my head, I couldn't help notice how jovial the driver was. How could a man, whose daily schedule was all but tedious to those who work in developed countries, be so apparently happy with life? The clichéd saying that "those less fortunate are always more grateful" was the first to surface, however, quietly dismissed.

Days passed and things were shaping up; visiting the prisons, house-house preaching, teaching Christianity in the markets, and interacting with the orphans were truly indescribable encounters. My most vivid memory was of the fete-like day held at the monastery – a fun day intended for poor-orphans. For them, soccer, singing and running were all but sufficient in amounting an enjoyable day. An excellent day, however, would include the attainment of a candy, a rare gift amongst the Kenyans, and so, we distributed one piece of candy per child. It was a physically and mentally demanding task, as kids had latched onto every visible surface of the body, while also aiming to ensure that each child only received one piece of candy so that all are recipients. As you would suspect, the supply had eventually depleted and all but one child was left candy-less. I had done my utmost efforts to console this child, but another child had provided the resolution: he selflessly offered to GIVE his candy to me so that I may hand it to the other orphan, a kind act done without grumbling and with Christ-like love.

Now, If you've read up to this point, you may think that all I've written is a nothing but a preplanned narrative with no direction, all strung together with a bunch of ordinary clichés, but here's the point: as Christians we ought to invest more back into God. As a child of God, each has his own figurative "candy," our desires, which God, the "candy" provider, freely supplies. Day after day, we latch onto Christ and plead for more, yet his distribution plan is thought-out and supersedes all human intellect. And although his supply is infinite, in what ever it may be, it serves a precise purpose – analogous to guaranteeing that all children receive a piece of candy. What differs between this giving child and the vast majority, is that most of us are unwilling to give back to God, the "candy" provider. You see, this child's willingness to potentiate the act of giving stems not only from seeing a brother in despair, but also from the knowledge that the candy provider freely gave and he freely received. And as the child offered the candy back to the provider, the provider can then administer his offering to the other child in need. We too, being recipients of God's freely given benefactions, must soften our hearts to give back to the Almighty so that he can use us to better his manifold. Further, a feeling of loss is not experienced whilst doing so, rather, immense joy, as to give to Christ is as giving yourself into your father's embrace. And as I compose this, I begin to realize why our airport escort was so joyous: he was encased in our Heavenly Father's embrace, as he reinvested the gift of driving given to him back into God and the service of His children. For those needing to witness a "candy-less" brother, just look around, for surely, there will always be a need for you to offer something God through someone around you.

But why all the complaints? The illustration of the complaining serves no other purpose than story dramatization and to illustrate that our ability to be grateful for God's endowments are consumed by our unwarranted complaints. Let me put it like this: if that child was not content with the acquisition of one candy, and greed captured his heart, his desire to reciprocate the act of giving would be non-existent. So, how can we offer to God and help His children, our brothers, with a grateful heart? Listen, I know all this stuff doesn't sound grand or theologically based as most spiritual pieces should be, what it is, as far as I can see, the fundamentals of ensuring a loving relationship with Christ. Therefore, despite our suboptimal jobs, our grumbles of "starvation" and first world problems, we ought to suppress our complaining nature, and in doing so, we may lovingly offer our gifts back to God and subsequently, his manifold.

MIRACLES IN PRISON

Missionary life in Africa is extremely blessed. For me it was a first time encounter with the uncontrollable, uncontainable, breath-taking flame of the Holy Spirit. A mission trip to Kenya under the guidance of Bishop Paul is like taking an aeroplane 2000 years into the past to meet the Apostles themselves. Worldly distractions are removed for you, and one is thrust thoroughly out of their comfort zone into the deep end – where Jesus calls us out by name to "come and see", to follow Him and spend time with Him unlike any other person in your life as a Christian. 21st Century meets the fiery first century Church. A scary reality is that the same God they experienced then is here. The same miracles, powerful prayers, fellowship and unity in the Spirit – this is all available to us right now. The same power that raised Christ from the dead lives in us always, it is up to us to nourish our spirit and be crucified to the world to share in His glorious resurrection. Mother Teresa once said "Stay where you are. Find your own Calcutta" – and she was right, the missionary work is cut out for us here in Australia, truly the harvest is great but the labourers are few. However, your time on a trip like this will serve to feed your spirit, to come to know the Son of God personally so you may go home and share Him with your family, your friends, your Church, your workplace and schools and with every creature who hungers.

One of the days Sayedna took our big group of Australians and Canadians to the Maximum Security prison at Kisumu. Upon entry we had to leave all phones, cameras and everything on the bus and write our names down just so the soldiers guarding the facility would be able to let us back out. It was massive, a large sandy land with the sun beating down on everyone inside. The first thing we noticed was a massive mosque to the left of the entrance, hundreds of Kenyan inmates sitting down in rows during a prayer. Their uniforms were black and white striped, fashioned straight out of the TV shows. The eyes of these men followed us closely as we walked through the complex, walking behind our fearless leader Bishop Paul. Their eyes seemed tired, undoubtedly they'd all had extremely unique journeys and tribulations in their lives, and some would be serving time until their last days on this earth.

We arrived into a central area; the prison inmates were working tirelessly in the background, moving heavy mattresses and cleaning the areas around the cells. We stopped, the Kenyan deacons with us began to set up the microphone system so that Sayedna could preach to the prisoners and we would afterwards have a chance to share with them and perform skits for them. It was boiling hot; our tongues began to stick to the dry roofs of our mouths as we waited for what felt like 20 minutes for the service to begin. Meanwhile the inmates gathered in front of us, a congregation of uniformed men, and some shirtless and bearing scars of their pasts. The deacons began singing some beautiful hymns in Swahili praising our Lord Jesus Christ, and to my amazement some of the prisoners came forward, took a microphone and joined in – leading their brothers in the audience in praise. There was no division between us and them, besides a few security guards with some bamboo sticks but I quickly realised these were men of Christ, we had nothing to fear. Bishop Paul's fiery faith and trust in Jesus was infectious. We stood with pride and watched, and joined in when we could.

Suddenly, the microphones started buzzing incessantly, and the deacons continued to sing without them. Sayedna beckoned a few of us to come over to the corner with him: "Boys! Come here ya shabab". I obeyed, making my way over with a few others where Sayedna huddled us together in a circle with him.

He explained to us so calmly "the demons are trying to make trouble for us ya shabab! We must pray! Yalla!" I had absolutely no idea what he meant by that or what was happening but I bowed my head. Bishop Paul began a beautiful prayer, asking our Lord Jesus Christ to be with us, and saying that this place is His, these people are His, and that they want to experience Jesus' love. He went on boldly, saying "the devil has no power here! Not authority here! Zis is YOUR place Lord!" and shortly after he concluded the prayer. The huddle split apart, and Sayedna walked over towards the microphone system. I turned my attention to speak to one of the boys for an instant, and heard in the background a massive surge in the system. It was a long and distinct buzzing sound, unlike before, and once it was over the previous buzzing stopped completely. The system was working fine again.

"Did you see that?!" One of the elder servants from Church came and asked excitedly. I asked him what on earth he was talking about. He explained that Sayedna walked over the sound system, and as he did he gave it a little flick using the Cross that was in his hand, and immediately the system roared and was working properly again. It took a moment to sink in. Had we just witnessed a miracle? And yet Sayedna was so calm about it as if it was nothing out of the ordinary? This was just a small example of Bishop Paul's faith, and the power of the Cross that conquered Satan completely. We had seen a miracle. We saw, as Sayedna prayed, our Lord making a way for us to share His name with others – and showing that there is no power over His Kingdom, the gates of Hades will never prevail over Jesus' name.

Upon witnessing this, many of us were hungry for more stories of the things Sayedna had seen in his years of missionary service. He gently said to us that this was nothing. He explained that if he went one day without seeing a miracle – that meant something was wrong. What a depth of a relationship with Jesus. If only all of us could have built this "best friend" relationship with the King of kings, our Saviour and our God.

At this point Sayedna left us, and went with Abouna Augustinos, Abouna Elisha and others to visit those on death row. Abouna Augustinos later said about these men: "They were more like angels then they were like men!" And was amazed to find a large picture of HH Pope Tawadros II in the death row section of the prison. We later found out that many of these prisoners do not get told the day in which they are sentenced and put to death. It is the worst kind of waiting game imaginable. To these men, not knowing the hour in which the Kingdom of Heaven will come takes on a different and very dark meaning.

Sayedna told us that on one of the recent visits before we had arrived to Africa, he had baptized about 40 of these faithful men into the Coptic Orthodox Church, and that sadly all of these had been executed a few weeks later. Abouna Augustinos said, "This is like pulling men out of the fire of hell, and straight into the Kingdom of Heaven!" And it was so true. This poignant story, although so sad, is a joyful one – that every day the blessed work of the missionaries is bringing the Gospel to many and drawing many hungry men and women to eternal life with our Lord.

> "Blessed are they who hunger and thirst for righteousness, for they shall be filled."

On our second return to the Prison, I experienced another amazing encounter that really touched me. We went in as before, this time with Copts from the Church in America having joined the group. A similar situation happened with the microphone system again, and after Sayedna prayed with us a very similar prayer it was functioning normally again. "Just incase you thought it was a fluke the first time!" the older servant said to me.

We had finished the service, skits included. A whole flock of inmates came up to us, we were shaking hands, greeting them with the few Swahili phrases we had picked out, and were giving out spiritual gifts, socks, clothing and whatever else we had to give. An individual approached one of our Kenyan priests, right next to me. He grabbed Abouna's arm and said something to him, as if he was pleading for his life. Abouna nodded a few times and the man walked away. "What did he say to you Abouna?" I was desperate to know, curiosity got the better of me. When I heard Abouna's answer my heart sunk. The man had asked Abouna for the Old Testament! He had managed to get the New Testament and had obviously read it and been touched by God's word, and he was so eager to finish the Bible, to have read the complete Word. I have never seen a hunger and thirst for God as great as this. It put me to complete shame. How many Bibles do we have in our homes, our churches and in our pockets on our phones, yet do we long to read it and feed from it as this man did? As St Peter said to Jesus, "You have the words of everlasting life." This is the nourishment for our soul, our means to hear God's voice in our lives and a lighthouse guiding us in our personal walk with Him.

ESCAPING THE GRIP OF DEATH

I had been in Kenya for a few months and I was debating within myself whether or not it was time to go home to Sydney or to continue with the mission. My visa was also approaching its expiration. At the time I was in Maseno, a village area where there is a Coptic compound consisting of a small hospital, theological college and beds for international missionaries. Maseno is about a 10-hour drive from Nairobi. I had decided that I would try and extend my visa so I went to the immigration office in the local major city of Kisumu. The servants who had lived in Kenya for a few years, told me to just let the immigration officers know that I was a servant and wanted to extend my visa, at which point they would just give me a stamp and I could be on my way. As I was entering the building I said a small prayer, "Lord, if you want me to continue on this mission so be it, and if you want me to return home so be it. Please just guide me to do what you want."

As I climbed the stairs to the immigration office, I could see a few tourists sitting in the plain white waiting area, frustrated as though they had been sitting there for quite some time. I hadn't even had the chance to fully walk in before a large African man with a deep voice spoke up "you, come with me." I looked around, his big pointing hand was aimed at my direction and no one else was in the vicinity...I knew he was talking to me so I approached. "come into my office" said the large immigration office. I began to follow him into his office. As I walked behind him I noticed the door of his office had a sign on the front that read, "Interrogation room" .... This was not good.

He stuck out his arm toward a rusting chair in front of his desk, he didn't open his mouth but his body language was commanding me to take a seat, so I did. "What are you here for?" the officer questioned. "I am just here to extend my visa. I am a servant." I said as instructed. The officer then took my passport and had a quick look, then moved from next to my chair to the other side of the desk facing me. SLAM!!! "I know who you are!" the officer said as he slammed my passport and his hands against the desk "you are a missionary from the Coptic church! You were previously at Kisumu church, Nyabera church, Ngombe church and Maseno church!" He was right. I had been to all those places. Now I know what you're thinking, I should now que a freak-out...however, I was totally calm. When on mission for God, you learn to completely and utterly depend on God. In Sydney, I don't doubt that if this happened, I would freak out, in fact anytime I get pulled over by the police for a random breath test I freak out, even though I know I didn't drink anything! Yet for some reason I knew that everything was in God's hands and I was at total peace. Being at total peace however, seemed to just make the officer angrier as I calmly looked at him and said, "yea, that's right, I was there." Infuriated at my response the officer then screamed louder and said, "I am going to fine you 50,000 shillings and throw you into prison, and there's nothing your embassy can do about it." I knew he was angry, and wanted a reaction, yet I didn't open my mouth. So the officer became even more enraged and yelled more threats until he seemed to get tired, and he sat down in his chair. Now have you ever done something you didn't realise was crazy until you looked back and thought "wow! That was crazy! I could've died!" que that moment...All of a sudden, with full confidence, I stood up, looked the officer in the face, took my passport off his desk, and calmly walked out of the building. Now any number of things would be running through a normal persons head right now, obvious things like; run! Or time to go back to Sydney! However, I felt my mission wasn't quite over yet, even though I very easily could have been arrested.

The problem was, I still needed to have my visa extended. So I called the church in Nairobi and mailed them my passport – yep, mail, another crazy moment. I wouldn't even trust Australian postal services with my passport let alone sub-Saharan African mail services. Yet I felt more as though I was trusting it into the hands of God's mail service and within a few days my passport had returned to me with an updated visa.

One week later, I had returned to the hospital compound in Maseno where I was staying. Walking in, a couple of the servants approached me giggling saying, "the police came here looking for you." Given they were giggling; I didn't think much of it so I went about my day as normal. About 1 month later, it was lent. Every weekday in lent we had set up for a liturgy to be prayed from 12pm-2pm, after which myself and the only other missionary there, would go out and greet the people, check up on the sick in the hospital and visit the locals. However, for some reason I felt that day God was telling me to go to my room, so I did. About an hour had passed and I got up to leave my room, however, about 3 or 4 steps away from the door, as I came to lift my legs to take my last steps out of the room, I froze. I can't fully explain what happened but I couldn't lift my legs. I felt as though there was a force keeping them down and pushing my chest from moving forward. It wasn't a painful feeling, it wasn't even some kind of nerve failure, I just couldn't move forward. I was still able though to walk around the room, I just couldn't exit. So I realised the Lord was not letting me leave. At the time I thought God just wanted me to spend some more quiet time with Him and not get too caught up in the service. About an hour later I felt a sudden rush, got up and walked out of my room as though nothing had happened.

Walking out I thought I caught hear people crying. Now having stayed at a hospital for some months now, I grew accustomed to loud cries, however, something was different about this cry, it sounded...angry. I continued to make my way to the main courtyard area, in front of the hospital, and found who was crying. It was a young man who had his working permit confiscated. I then noticed more people crying, some also had their workers permit confiscated, others had their passports taken and all were issued court orders. "How dare he does this!" said the young man who had his workers permit taken, "He cannot do this!" "who?" I asked, "who did this?" "It was that immigration officer!" answered a local servant, "That same officer, who has been trying to get you for the last month or so. He came with a whole patrol! How did he not find you?"

I didn't answer, I didn't know what to say, how do you explain that God was stepping on my feet not letting me leave my room? I was too stuck on the question. "This doesn't make sense! What is this guy's problem? Why was this immigration guy so intent on getting me?"

Then Lauwie, one of the local Kenyan servants pulled me aside and said, "Do you know that immigration officer? He isn't just an immigration officer, he is a Somalian muslim who we believe has ties to El Shebab (the terrorist organisation)". Now it was beginning to make sense. Lauwie further explained that this man wanted to arrest me and make an example of me. I paused..."That's awesome! I get to be arrested for Christ? Go tell him to come back!" I had long heard of people who had been arrested for Christ's sake and thought I would have the honour of being counted amongst them. "No!" Lauwie shouted, "I know what you're thinking, stay in jail for a few days, then you'll be let free, but this guy is a terrorist! Who knows what he will do to you, plus think about the effects your imprisonment will have on the mission..." He was right, I did only think I would be in jail for a couple of days, and who knows what this guy was capable of and the implications on the mission. "So what are my options?" I said, knowing full well what my only real option was. "You need to escape" answered Lauwie, "wait until early morning then take the hospital vehicle and sneak away to the airport and fly back to Nairobi." So that night I said my goodbyes to all I could, packed my bags. Early the next morning, one of the hospital drivers came to my room and we began to proceed to the car park. As we came to our vehicle, for some reason it wouldn't start. We then tried to locate the other vehicle but someone had already taken it out, the only vehicle left was the ambulance. So I packed my bags and around 5:30am we drove out of the complex, to the airport and safely arrived in Nairobi. Later that day I called the Maseno complex to see how everything had gone that day. As I was speaking to one of the servants I asked if that immigration officer had returned looking for me. "He did!" she replied, "he came about 2 hours after you left." "Lucky Africans don't wake up early" I joked, she then laughed and said, "Actually, he was waiting outside all night and all morning for you, hiding in the bushes, just in case you tried to escape. He checked every vehicle that was coming in and out of the hospital, from cars to bicycles. The thing is, the only vehicles they are not allowed to check are ambulance vehicles..."

I hear this man no longer has his job but even if he does, it is good for people to know that God is always looking out for them. It may not be as obvious as it is in the mission fields, but trust God, He has you covered, even if the situation is as grim and unshakable as this, He has your back.

THE ORPHANS

GOD, love, education, shelter and food... 5 essential elements to living; this is exactly what is provided at the Raha Kids orphanage in Nairobi, Kenya. Upon our visitation on the 4th of July, 2014, St Marks Coptic Orthodox church youth were privileged to meet and make friendships with the children at Raha kids. As we walked in, I felt a gush of love sweep over me; I could honestly feel the love and dedication towards this service. These children were served by a Coptic nun, who gave each child a piece of her heart daily. Entering the classrooms and observing their learning style, was truly eye opening! The love between the children themselves, truly allowed us to observe the simple love we are required to show towards God. Struggling with one another to answer simple mathematics questions, sounding out a word letter by letter, in one voice and listening attentively, whilst a picture book was being read to them. We were then asked to present a short biblical story in the form of a play. My group was blessed with the opportunity to tell the story of Zacchaeus- perfect for a 5-7 aged male audience. Their simplicity, willingness to hear the word of God and their undivided attention was insightful to observe! After thoroughly enjoying our comedic presentation, they decided to share with us a song they were taught about Zacchaeus. Together we sang the story, with the appropriate actions. The smiling faces of the boys in that classroom are now imprinted in my mind. Afterward, being able to interact with them on a personal level was the perfect opportunity to observe the hand of God working miracles with His children. I approached a boy, sitting alone and decided to chat with him. Sitting beside this 6year old boy, Fidel, I was able to listen to his story and understand how he arrived to become a 'Raha Kid'. I knew this little boy, had been touched by the hand of God- being picked off the streets, after being abandoned by his parents. Raha kids gave him God, a home, a family— Hope. As we prayed quietly together, Fidel truly opened my eyes to the simplicity of the heart of a child. Immediately the verse came to my mind " Assuredly, I say to you, unless you are converted and become as little children, you will by no means enter the kingdom of heaven." [Matthew 18:3]. It is then that I came to the realisation that this is ALL we are required to do. Come to the God, as a child to their father; leaving everything in our lives in His more than capable hands. We, like Fidel, should never doubt the power of our Almighty God. If a 6 year old boy could submit his life in the hands of God, we could too!

RESURRECTION GARDEN

In a country like Australia where one is occupied and overwhelmed with work, education, time and money, it is difficult to attain some time alone, where you displace yourself from the world and all it's superficial distractions. During our short stay in Nairobi, bishop Paul invited us to visit a spiritual garden in the midst of a monastery named the Resurrection Garden. A garden with vintage landscapes solely hand built and maintained by the servants of the monastery. It was amazing to see the service that these people provided and the outcome of their work, their tireless efforts was a clear indication of the hand of God. Just as Hebrews 6:10 mentions:

"For God is not unjust to forget your work and labor

of love which you have shown toward His name, in that you have ministered to the saints, and do minister".
(Hebrews 6:10)

The resurrection Garden was a place that gave us the opportunity to sit alone beside God and truly talk to him. Each one of us had their own space, being surrounded with statues, monuments and powerful verses from the bible. Sitting alone in such a spiritual place taught us how important it is to have quiet time. You don't notice how much time and effort you are wasting on superficial worldly desires and actions until you get a taste of real quiet time. Which is not just 15 minutes you spend every night before going to sleep but an entire day's worth of spiritual intake, where you learn not only of the word and your spirituality but also about yourself, what your faults in life are, your strengths, weaknesses and how you should solely focus on yourself before observing everyone around you.

AFRICAN SAFARI

Joyful singing and bright smiles were not the only way we saw the beauty of God in Kenya. Our safari trip reminded us of our mighty Lord as we drove through the wild plains to spot the different animals of His creation. We took a two-day trip amongst the busy schedule of service to be reminded of the splendour of creation and the perfect order of God's handiwork. Separated into groups we spent the two days in a mini bus with our driver. The roofs opened up so that we were able to stand and have a perfect 360-degree angle of the land and animals. In awe we saw creatures we knew and ones we didn't.

When we would look around us, we would see how small we were compared to not only some of the elephants but also the land. Our bus took such a minute part in an incomprehensibly boundless terrain. From our position on the bus where we stood as observers of this great creation, we were reminded of the intricacy and detail in which our Lord fashioned us. We saw how animals lived together as herds to protect each other, how elephants protected their babies, how giraffes majestically ran through the plains and how zebras were created with perfect stripes to live through the African terrain. We saw waterholes for drinking and carcasses that animals had fed on - all of which showed us that nature worked in a perfect cycle. Each animal had their needs met and had different talents/characteristics to enable their survival. Truly we were reminded that if the Lord can feed the sparrows of the air and provide the cows with food to feed on then how much more are we loved by our Father, and how much more will we be provided for.

SPONTANEOUS ENGAGEMENT

During our time in Maseno, our group was blessed with the opportunity to witness the application of many of the church sacraments including baptisms, communion, anointment of the sick and more. One of the most beautiful experiences we had regarding these Sacraments was the ordination of the new Kenyan Priest, Father Tadros. The blessing that was Father Tadros remained with us for the rest of our time in Maseno as he continued to reside in the monastery and serve alongside us for the duration of our stay. It fuelled the fire within all of us to see the fiery Spirit with which he served with following his decision to surrender his life to God and serve Him full-time in Africa.

Inspired by the Spirit of Africa, two members of our group decided to celebrate their engagement to one another while we stayed in Maseno. The celebration was conducted in true African way with the fiery chanting that we became so accustomed to. No doubt, they as well as us, will remember this special occasion for the rest of our lives.

COW DUNG HUTS

On the 2nd day of our Safari trip, we visited the Masai Mara tribe, a local tribe within the region of Kenya that occupied our safari tour. To many of us, it was the first time to see a native tribe who solely depended on the land where agriculture was a major part of their lives. The women and men, with dancing, singing and chanting in their native tongue, greeted us with traditional songs. A traditional dance by the males required them to jump to a certain height and the higher they jump, the more wife's and livestock they were entitled to. Our priest, Father Mark, partook in this activity to see how he competed against the locals. Needless to say, he was entitled to a chicken leg in comparison to the many cows that the locals jumped for. We then split into many groups where we given private tours of the compound, huts and their workshops. As we walked, we saw children who would have a swarm of flies near their eyes and not even annoyed in the slightest to swat them away. These children wore hardly any clothes and were living in dirty conditions. Their huts were made of cow dung and were no bigger than a few meters squared. Due to the components of the huts, they smelled terrible and left a foul stench within the hut, and also in the compound. The huts were extremely small and fit more people than our huge houses would fit, approximately six people per family. In our eyes, the natives lived very primitively and we felt sorry for them and the way they lived. But they were constantly smiling. The children were always smiling and always wanted to play. The native men and women smiled and waved at us as we walked by. The Masai Mara tribe happily lived this way and this was the only way they knew. They had nothing but were happy which also served as a huge lesson to us who always seek the materialistic pleasures of this world to give us happiness. They used the resources in the land available by God, and made the most of it, and lived fulfilling lives. The male tribe member explained to us that they drink the blood of cows mixed with milk in order to provide sustenance and for them to feel full. This was a truly remarkable tribe and demonstrated to most of us, the uselessness and emptiness of materialistic pleasures. They talk us a lesson that in order to be happy, you don't need worldly pleasures. We thank God that He has presented us with the opportunity to visit the Masai Mara tribe and that this experience has taught us a valuable lesson.

MOUNTAIN CLIMB

"His foundation is in the holy mountains"
– Psalm 87:1

When climbing up a mountain, getting to the top is the most difficult exercise. At the top however, when you encounter The Lord, the journey fades into a distant memory. Sometimes we fell but as we do in all our lives, we picked ourselves back up, despite the many obstacles on the way. A lot of people were walking up the same mountain, a narrow path we maneuvered through to get to the top, and so we tried to encourage each other, tried to stay focused and bring everyone else with us. Assisted those who were struggling and help direct those who go astray and lost their way up the mountain. The narrow path - we had to keep our eyes focused on the top. Using the strength God gave us to help each other get back up and reach the top! Everyone sharing the one common goal - to experience God and His fullness at the top of that mountain through time spent in quietness with Him. There were thorns on the way that poked us and discouraged us but we leant on those around us for strength, reminding us all of the power of fellowship in life. Leaving the mountain was difficult. Leaving that beautiful, peace- filled place where God's glory shone. Where it was just you and God. Being witnesses to his perfect creation from the mountaintop and feeling His word encapsulate us. But just as Moses who spent time with God upon the mount of Sinai, we left there with a better understanding of God's plan, knowing the feeling of his presence and yearning to share it with the rest of His children at the bottom. No matter our struggles and tribulations when we come down to the world we know that we will get through them because we have been to that mountain top and witnessed His glory! You learn that everything you do in life should ultimately be to get you closer up that mountaintop to feel Him. All should be done for His glory!

SHARING JESUS

House visitations allowed us an opportunity to take God's Word straight to the homes of the Kenyan people. We entered each house praying and knowing:

"But now, o Lord, You are our Father; We are the clay and You our potter; And all we are the work of Your hand." (Isaiah 64:8)

We were there to share God's word through the power of the Spirit. No two visitations were the same. Sometimes we stopped for a short prayer; sometimes a simple song; we shared contemplations from the Holy Bible (both the youth and the Kenyans); we even met and spoke with people on the roads between houses. One thing did remain the same however - each visit allowed us to share in the fellowship of Christ. We did not enter their homes to 'teach' or 'preach' (they had more spiritual nourishment to offer us) but to share in this blessed fellowship of Christ. In this fellowship we came to know some of the Kenyans more intimately. They spoke with us about their sufferings and their joy; their failings and their redemption; their lacking and their blessings; their dreams and desires. And in their stories we came to know the simplicity, love and hope rooted in the blessed Kenyan people's faith. I'll finish with some wisdom shared with us at the end of one of our visitations. When we asked our host if he had any prayer requests he replied: 'Everybody has a request for God... Gods knows what we need from him and what is best. Just pray without request and God will provide.'

THE BOOK OF ACTS RE-LIVED

I remember the day so clearly, perhaps more clearly than any of the other days. I remember in the morning, being told that today would be a special day, but really not wanting to go, not feeling like I had enough energy for yet another big day and just wanting to stay home and sleep. I would never have expected the day God had planned for us.

So, as per usual, we were out of the monastery and on the bus by about 9:00am. Once we had arrived in the church, we walked in to such a beautiful scene. A primitive looking, yet beautiful church, almost full before the mass had even started. Women and children were singing and praising God so fervently. This scene in itself was heaven. It was even shameful! Their eagerness to praise God, their punctuality and their desire. This was God's day to them, and they honored that with all their heart and being.

We were told that a few families from the village were going to be baptized and so the baptisms begun. Family after family coming up and professing their faith in Jesus Christ. Children, women, men, babies, teenagers, the whole lot. The line seemed never ending. It was like an 'express' baptism. One abouna at the baptismal font doing the dunking, the next abouna anointing the holy mayroon and so on. There would have been over 100 people baptized. There was one woman who was over 95 years old who couldn't get into the baptismal font without Abouna carrying her! I was standing next to abouna in the baptismal font and I cannot describe the amount of abounding joy and peace I felt. I could not keep the smile off my face at the prospect of how many people's names were being written in the book of life and how present the Holy Spirit was, entering into everyone being baptized. I saw the body of Christ growing like I had never seen before. It was the most joyful I have ever felt and it brought me to tears. These people BELIEVED in Christ's atoning sacrifice. They craved freedom, forgiveness, a protector, a comforter. And let me tell you, despite every single one of them going into the baptismal a little frightened at the prospect of being dunked in three times, every single woman/man/child came out with peace and a freedom on their faces. I don't really think words can describe it, but I could certainly feel it.

The rest of the mass continued and the church was so full! People were sitting on the ground! I remember I was standing up, and one woman from the church, grabbed a few children off the bench so I could sit down. I was so overwhelmed with this act of kindness and love. This woman truly had the love of God in her heart. How many times do I go to church, and see all the people at the back standing and offer my seat for them? I was so ashamed!

When the mass finished, Bishop Paul made an announcement, along the lines of: "Anyone who feels affected by the magic that is being done in the village, or if you fear it, or want to stop it, come up to the front, and we will pray for you". I didn't really expect some people to come up to the front, but almost half the church came. I saw in this act, a desire for freedom, a hatred of this magic, and I once again felt ashamed, at this act of true repentance. How often do I, admit a hatred of my sin, and crave the freedom that only our God can provide for us.

This would have had to be the happiest day on the trip for me. Never in my life have I felt so much joy, and I honestly think that this joy came from the celebration that was happening in heaven. It made me realize that

I needed more of this joy in my life. More joy in Christ's atoning sacrifice, and His resurrection. More joy in the fact that we have FREEDOM. We have a protector and a comforter. We are the Body of Christ here on earth. We NEED to 'live out' our baptism. I also believe that everyone gained something completely different from the day, each a gift and a message so special, from God himself. I feel extremely blessed to have been a part of such a day.

ELEVENTH HOUR SALVATION

The prison experience was a highlight for many of the youth on this Kenyan mission trip. On the trip the previous year, Father Augustinos had remarked: "The men were more like angels than prisoners!" and this definitely held true this year. By the grace of God, the Holy Spirit directed our fathers, elder servants and a number of the young boys to speak and preach the Gospel and God's love to the inmates of Kisumu Maximum Security Prison and Siaya Medium Security Prison. Their angelic nature was revealed in how deeply the word of God cut them to the heart, and how happily they received it.

In Kisumu prison, one of the first things to be noticed

was how a few of the men had their own Swahili Bibles. This gave me great joy as the previous year one of the inmates had very strongly pleaded with one of the Kenyan priests to provide Bibles. God's hand was beautifully shown in filling that hunger for righteousness. Truly freedom comes in Christ as St Paul wrote in Romans 6.

A notable event in this prison was the amazing wonder God worked in approximately 70 prisoners being baptised and given Holy Communion by Bishop Paul and fathers Augustinos and Mark. About 30 of these men were on death row. This was beautiful encapsulated by one of the youth sharing the story of the Right Hand Thief – an eleventh hour salvation story that was poignantly relevant to the men literally coming to Christ at that very moment. The prison warren was so moved he even took to the microphone to implore the men to listen to our speakers, and accept Christ into their hearts. To see the apostolic ministry unfolding in this powerful way was truly amazing. Truly God hungers after each soul to be saved and it was an extreme blessing to witness.

In Siaya prison, the story of our Lord and Saviour Jesus Christ promising the Right Thief salvation was again shared among others; again the Spirit moved the hearts of many prisoners, and a large number of them accepted to be prayed for by father Jacob and the mission group. During this prayer, the repentant hearts of the prisoners were so beautifully visible, with some praying with tears, beating on their chests and kneeling down before the Lord, asking their lives to be changed. The presence of our Lord was so thick and tangible during this time, a few of the youth were truly touched to the core.

To top of this amazing experience, we had an unreal opportunity to play a soccer match with the prisoners. Following the warden's permission, a makeshift field was erected out of nowhere and a brother translator made a very entertaining commentary on the lively match. It was an unbelievable fellowship experience, brothers in Christ together and He was truly glorified by that day's events.

www.ingramcontent.com/pod-product-compliance
Lightning Source LLC
LaVergne TN
LVHW091308080426
835510LV00007B/408